THE WAY OF

The Way of Man

According to
The Teaching of
HASIDISM

By

Martin Buber

THE CITADEL PRESS
Secaucus, New Jersey

FIRST PUBLISHED IN ENGLAND 1950
BY ROUTLEDGE & KEGAN PAUL LTD
SECOND IMPRESSION 1963
PUBLISHED BY
VINCENT STUART PUBLISHERS LTD
45 LOWER BELGRAVE STREET
LONDON SW1

Sixth paperbound printing

Citadel Press, Inc., Publishers
A subsidiary of Lyle Stuart, Inc.
120 Enterprise Avenue, Secaucus, N.J. 07094

ISBN 0-8065-0024-7

PRE

PREFACE

The name 'hasidism' (in Hebrew *hasidut*, i.e., originally, 'allegiance' and hence, 'piety') designates a mystical-religious movement which seized Eastern European Jewry about the middle of the 18th century and numbers many congregations to this day.*

In most systems of belief the believer considers that he can achieve a perfect relationship to God by renouncing the world of the senses and overcoming his own natural being. Not so the hasid. Certainly, 'cleaving' unto God is to him the highest aim of the human person, but to achieve it he is not required to abandon the external and internal reality of earthly being, but to affirm it in its true, God-oriented essence and thus so to transform it that he can offer it up to God.

Hasidism is no pantheism. It teaches the absolute transcendence of God, but as combined with his conditioned immanence. The world is an irradiation of God, but as it is endowed with an independence of existence and striving, it is apt, always and everywhere, to form a crust around itself. Thus, a divine spark lives in every thing and being, but each such spark is enclosed by an isolating shell. Only man can liberate it and re-join it with the Origin: by holding holy converse with the thing and using it in a holy manner, that is, so that his intention in doing so remains

* Compare on this my books *Hasidism* (New York, 1948) and *Tales of the Hasidim* (2 volumes, New York, 1947 and 1948: Thames and Hudson 1956).

directed towards God's transcendence. Thus the divine immanence emerges from the exile of the 'shells'.

But also in man, in every man, is a force divine. And in man far more than in all other beings it can pervert itself, can be misused by himself. This happens if he, instead of directing it towards its origin, allows it to run directionless and seize at everything that offers itself to it; instead of hallowing passion, he makes it evil. But here, too, a way to redemption is open: he who with the entire force of his being 'turns' to God, lifts at this his point of the universe the divine immanence out of its debasement, which he has caused.

The task of man, of every man, according to hasidic teaching, is to affirm for God's sake the world and himself and by this very means to transform both.

CONTENTS

THE WAY OF MAN

THE
WAY OF MAN
ACCORDING TO THE TEACHING
OF HASIDISM

I. HEART-SEARCHING

Rabbi Shneur Zalman, The Rav[1] of Northern White Russia (died 1813), was put in jail in Petersburg, because the mitnagdim[2] had denounced his principles and his way of living to the government. He was awaiting trial when the chief of the gendarmes entered his cell. The majestic and quiet face of the rav, who was so deep in meditation that he did not at first notice his visitor, suggested to the chief, a thoughtful person, what manner of man he had before him. He began to converse with his prisoner and brought up a number of questions which had occurred to him in reading the Scriptures. Finally he asked: 'How are we to understand that God, the all-knowing, said to Adam: " Where art thou?" '

'Do you believe,' answered the rav, 'that the Scriptures are eternal and that every era, every generation and every man is included in them?'

[1] Rabbi.   [2] i.e., adversaries (of Hasidism).

'I believe this,' said the other.

'Well then,' said the zaddik,[1] 'in every era, God calls to every man: "Where are you in your world? So many years and days of those allotted to you have passed, and how far have you gotten in your world?" God says something like this: "You have lived forty-six years. How far along are you?" '

When the chief of the gendarmes heard his age mentioned, he pulled himself together, laid his hand on the rav's shoulder, and cried: 'Bravo!' But his heart trembled.

What happens in this tale?

At first sight, it reminds us of certain Talmudic stories in which a Roman or some other heathen questions a Jewish sage about a biblical passage with a view to exposing an alleged contradiction in Jewish religious doctrine, and receives a reply which either explains that there is no such contradiction or refutes the questioner's arguments in some other way; sometimes, a personal admonition is added to the actual reply. But we soon perceive an important difference between those Talmudic stories and this hasidic one, though at first the difference appears greater than it actually is. It consists in the fact that in the hasidic story the reply is given on a different plane from that on which the question is asked.

The chief wants to expose an alleged contradiction in Jewish doctrine. The Jews profess to believe in God

[1] i.e., proved true; so the leaders of the Hasidic communities are called.

as the all-knowing, but the Bible makes him ask questions as they are asked by someone who wants to learn something he does not know. God seeks Adam, who has hidden himself. He calls into the garden, asking where he is; it would thus seem that he does not know it, that it is possible to hide from him, and consequently, that he is not all-knowing. Now, instead of explaining the passage and solving the seeming contradiction, the rabbi takes the text merely as a starting-point from where he proceeds to reproach the chief with his past life, his lack of seriousness, his thoughtlessness and irresponsibility. An impersonal question which, however seriously it may be meant in the present instance, is in fact no genuine question but merely a form of controversy, calls forth a personal reply, or rather, a personal admonition in lieu of a reply. It thus seems as if nothing had remained of those Talmudic answers but the admonition which sometimes accompanied them.

But let us examine the story more closely. The chief inquires about a passage from the biblical story of Adam's sin. The rabbi's answer means, in effect: 'You yourself are Adam, you are the man whom God asks: "Where art thou?"' It would thus seem that the answer gives no explanation of the passage as such. In fact, however, it illuminates both the situation of the biblical Adam and that of every man in every time and in every place. For as soon as the chief hears and understands that the biblical question is addressed to him, he is bound to realize what it means when God asks: 'Where art thou?', whether the question be addressed to Adam or to some other man. In so asking, God does not expect to learn something he does not know; what he wants is to produce an effect in man which can only be produced by just such a question, provided that it reaches man's heart—that man allows it to reach his heart.

Adam hides himself to avoid rendering accounts, to escape responsibility for his way of living. Every man hides for this purpose, for every man is Adam and finds himself in Adam's situation. To escape responsibility for his life, he turns existence into a system of hideouts. And in thus hiding again and again 'from the face of God', he enmeshes himself more and more deeply in perversity. A new situation thus arises, which becomes more and more questionable with every day, with every new hideout. This situation can be precisely defined as follows: Man cannot escape the eye of God, but in trying to hide from him, he is hiding from himself. True, in him too there is something that seeks him, but he makes it harder and harder for that 'something' to find him. This question is designed to awaken man and destroy his system of hideouts; it is to show man to what pass he has come and to awake in him the great will to get out of it.

Everything now depends on whether man faces the question. Of course, every man's heart, like that of the chief in the story, will tremble when he hears it. But his system of hideouts will help him to overcome this emotion. For the Voice does not come in a thunderstorm which threatens man's very existence; it is a 'still small voice', and easy to drown. So long as this is done, man's life will not become a *way*. Whatever success and enjoyment he may achieve, whatever power he may attain and whatever deeds he may do, his life will remain way-less, so long as he does not face the Voice. Adam faces the Voice, perceives his enmeshment, and avows: 'I hid myself'; this is the beginning of man's way. The decisive heart-searching is the beginning of the way in man's life; it is, again and again, the beginning of a human way. But heart-searching is decisive only if it leads to the way. For there is a sterile kind of heart-searching, which leads to nothing but self-torture, despair and still deeper enmeshment. When the Rabbi of Ger,[1] in expounding the Scriptures, came to the words which Jacob addresses to his servant: 'When Esau my brother meets thee, and asks thee, saying, Whose art thou? and whither goest thou? and whose are these before thee?', he would say to his disciples: 'Mark well how similar Esau's questions are to the saying of our sages: "Consider three things. Know whence you came, whither you are going, and to whom you will have to render accounts." Be very careful, for great caution should be exercised by him who considers these three things: lest Esau ask in him. For Esau, too, may ask these questions and bring man into a state of gloom.'

There is a demonic question, a spurious question, which apes God's question, the question of Truth. Its

[1] i.e., Góra Kalwarya near Warsaw.

13

characteristic is that it does not stop at: 'Where art thou?', but continues: 'From where you have got to, there is no way out.' This is the wrong kind of heart-searching, which does not prompt man to turn, and put him on the way, but, by representing turning as hopeless, drives him to a point where it appears to have become entirely impossible and man can go on living only by demonic pride, the pride of perversity.

II. THE PARTICULAR WAY

Rabbi Baer of Radoshitz once said to his teacher, the 'Seer' of Lublin: 'Show me one general way to the service of God.'

The zaddik replied: 'It is impossible to tell men what way they should take. For one way to serve God is through learning, another through prayer, another through fasting, and still another through eating. Everyone should carefully observe what way his heart draws him to, and then choose this way with all his strength.'

In the first place, this story tells us something about our relationship to such genuine service as was performed by others before us. We are to revere it and learn from it, but we are not to imitate it. The great and holy deeds done by others are examples for us, since they show, in a concrete manner, what greatness and holiness is, but they are not models which we should copy. However small our achievements may be in comparison with those of our forefathers, they have their real value in that we bring them about in our own way and by our own efforts.

The maggid[1] of Zlotchov[2] was asked by a hasid: 'We are told: "Everyone in Israel is in duty bound to say: When will my work approach the works of my fathers, Abraham, Isaac and Jacob?" How are we to understand this? How could we ever venture to think that we could do what our fathers did?'

[1] i.e., preacher.   [2] Town in Eastern Galicia.

The rabbi expounded: 'Just as our fathers founded new ways of serving, each a new service according to his character: one the service of love, the other that of stern justice, the third that of beauty, so each one of us in his own way shall devise something new in the light of teachings and of service, and do what has not yet been done.'

Every person born into this world represents something new, something that never existed before, something original and unique. 'It is the duty of every person in Israel to know and consider that he is unique in the world in his particular character and that there has never been anyone like him in the world, for if there had been someone like him, there would have been no need for him to be in the world. Every single man is a new thing in the world, and is called upon to fulfil his particularity in this world. For verily: that this is not done, is the reason why the coming of the Messiah is delayed.' Every man's foremost task is the actualization of his unique, unprecedented and never-recurring potentialities, and not the repetition of something that another, and be it even the greatest, has already achieved.

The wise Rabbi Bunam once said in old age, when he had already grown blind: 'I should not like to change places with our father Abraham! What good would it do God if Abraham became like blind Bunam, and blind Bunam became like Abraham? Rather than have this happen, I think I shall try to become a little more myself.'

The same idea was expressed with even greater pregnancy by Rabbi Zusya when he said, a short while before his death: 'In the world to come I shall not be asked: "Why were you not Moses?" I shall be asked: "Why were you not Zusya?" '

We are here confronted with a doctrine which is based on the fact that men are essentially unlike one another, and which therefore does not aim at making them alike. All men have access to God, but each man has a different access. Mankind's great chance lies precisely in the unlikeness of men, in the unlikeness of their qualities and inclinations. God's all-inclusiveness manifests itself in the infinite multiplicity of the ways that lead to him, each of which is open to one man. When some disciples of a deceased zaddik came to the 'Seer' of Lublin and expressed surprise at the fact that his customs were different from those of their late master, the 'Seer' exclaimed: 'What sort of God would that be who has only one way in which he can be served!' But by the fact that each man, starting from his particular place and in a manner determined by his particular nature, is able to reach God, God can be reached by mankind as such, through its multiple advance by all those different ways.

God does not say: 'This way leads to me and that does not', but he says: 'Whatever you do may be a way to me, provided you do it in such a manner that it leads you to me.' But what it is that can and shall be done by just this person and no other, can be revealed to him only in himself. In this matter, as I said before it would only be misleading to study the achievements of another man and endeavour to equal him; for in so doing, a man would miss precisely what he and he alone is called upon to do. The Baal-Shem[1] said: 'Every man should behave according to his "rung". If he does not, if he seizes the "rung" of a fellow-man and abandons his own, he will actualize neither the one nor the other.' Thus, the way by which a man can reach God is revealed to him only through the knowledge of his own being, the knowledge of his essential quality and inclination. 'Everyone has in him something precious that is in no one else.' But this precious something in a man is revealed to him only if he truly perceives his strongest feeling, his central wish, that in him which stirs his inmost being.

Of course, in many cases, a man knows this his strongest feeling only in the shape of a particular passion, of the 'Evil Urge' which seeks to lead him astray. Naturally, a man's most powerful desire, in seeking satisfaction, rushes in the first instance at objects which lie across his path. It is necessary, therefore, that the power of even this feeling, of even this impulse, be diverted from the casual to the essential, and from the relative to the absolute. Thus a man finds his way.

A zaddik once said: 'At the end of Ecclesiastes we read: "At the end of the matter, the whole is heard: Fear God." Whatever matter you follow to its end, there, at the end, you will hear one thing: "Fear God",

[1] i.e., Master of the Name (of God). So the founder of Hasidism, Rabbi Israel ben Eliezer (1700-1760), was surnamed.

and this one thing is the whole. There is no thing in the world which does not point a way to the fear of God and to the service of God. Everything is commandment.' By no means, however, can it be our true task in the world into which we have been set, to turn away from the things and beings that we meet on our way and that attract our hearts; our task is precisely to get in touch, by hallowing our relationship with them, with what manifests itself in them as beauty, pleasure, enjoyment. Hasidism teaches that rejoicing in the world, if we hallow it with our whole being, leads to rejoicing in God.

One point in the tale of the 'Seer' seems to contradict this, namely, that among the examples of 'ways' we find not only eating but also fasting. But if we consider this in the general context of hasidic teaching, it appears that though detachment from nature, abstinence from natural life, may, in the cases of some men mean the necessary starting-point of their 'way' or, perhaps, a necessary act of self-isolation at certain crucial moments of existence, it may never mean the whole way. Some men must begin by fasting, and begin by it again and again, because it is peculiar to them that only by asceticism can they achieve liberation from their enslavement to the world, deepest heart-searching and ultimate communion with the Absolute. But never should asceticism gain mastery over a man's life. A man may only detach himself from nature in order to revert to it again and, in hallowed contact with it, find his way to God.

The biblical passage which says of Abraham and the three visiting angels: 'And he stood over them under the tree and they did eat' is interpreted by Rabbi Zusya to the effect that man stands above the angels, because he knows something unknown to them, namely, that eating may be hallowed by the eater's intention. Through Abraham the angels, who were unaccustomed to eating, participated in the intention by which he used to dedicate it to God. Any natural act, if hallowed, leads to God, and nature needs man for what no angel can perform on it, namely, its hallowing.

III. RESOLUTION

A hasid of the Rabbi of Lublin once fasted from one Sabbath to the next. On Friday afternoon he began to suffer such cruel thirst that he thought he would die. He saw a well, went up to it, and prepared to drink. But instantly he realized that because of the one brief hour he had still to endure, he was about to destroy the work of the entire week. He did not drink and went away from the well. Then he was touched by a feeling of pride for having passed this difficult test. When he became aware of it, he said to himself, 'Better I go and drink than let my heart fall prey to pride.' He went back to the well, but just as he was going to bend down to draw water, he noticed that his thirst had disappeared. When the Sabbath had begun, he entered his teacher's house. 'Patchwork!' the rabbi called to him, as he crossed the threshold.

When in my youth I heard this tale for the first time, I was struck by the harsh manner in which the master treats his zealous disciple. The latter makes his utmost efforts to perform a difficult feat of asceticism. He feels tempted to break off and overcomes the temptation, but his only reward, after all his trouble, is an expression of disapproval from his teacher. It is true that the disciple's first inhibition was due to the power of the body over the soul, a power which had still to be broken, but the second sprung from a truly noble motive: better to fail than, for the sake of succeeding,

21

fall prey to pride. How can a man be scolded for such an inner struggle? Is this not asking too much of a man?

Long afterwards (but still as early as a quarter of a century ago), when I myself retold this tale from tradition, I understood that there was no question here of something being asked of a man. The zaddik of Lublin was no friend of asceticism, and the hasid's fast was certainly not designed to please him, but to lift the hasid's soul to a higher 'rung'; the Seer himself had admitted that fasting could serve this purpose in the initial stage of a person's development and also later, at critical moments of his life. What the master—apparently after watching the progress of the venture with true understanding—says to the disciple, means undoubtedly: 'This is not the proper manner to attain a higher rung'. He warns the disciple of something that perforce hinders him from achieving his purpose. What this is, becomes clear enough. The object of the reproof is the advance and subsequent retreat; it is the wavering, shilly-shallying character of the man's doing that makes it questionable. The opposite of 'patchwork' is work 'all of a piece'. Now how does one achieve work 'all of a piece?' Only with a united soul.

Again we are troubled by the question whether this man is not being treated too harshly. As things are in this world, one man—'by nature' or 'by grace', however one chooses to put it—has a unitary soul, a soul all of a piece, and accordingly performs unitary works, works all of a piece, because his soul, by being as it is, prompts and enables him to do so; another man has a divided, complicated, contradictory soul, and this, naturally, affects his doings: their inhibitions and disturbances originate in the inhibitions and disturbances of his soul; its restlessness is expressed in their restlessness. What else can a man so constituted do than try to overcome the temptations which approach him on the way to what is, at a given time, his goal? What else can he do than each time, in the middle of his doing, 'pull himself together', as we say, that is, rally his vacillating soul, and again and again, having rallied it, re-concentrate it upon the goal—and moreover be ready, like the hasid in the story when pride touches him, to sacrifice the goal in order to save the soul?

Only when, in the light of these questions, we subject our story to renewed scrutiny, do we apprehend the teaching implied in the Seer's criticism. It is the teaching that a man can unify his soul. The man with the divided, complicated, contradictory soul is not helpless: the core of his soul, the divine force in its depths, is capable of acting upon it, changing it, binding the conflicting forces together, amalgamating the diverging elements—is capable of unifying it. This unification must be accomplished *before* a man undertakes some unusual work. Only with a united soul will he be able so to do it that it becomes not patchwork but work all of a piece. The Seer thus reproaches the hasid with having embarked on his venture without first unifying his soul; unity of soul can never be achieved in the middle of the work. Nor should it be supposed that it can be brought about by asceticism; asceticism can purify, concentrate, but it cannot preserve its achievements intact until the attainment of the goal—it cannot protect the soul from its own contradiction.

One thing must of course not be lost sight of: unification of the soul is never final. Just as a soul most unitary from birth is sometimes beset by inner difficulties, thus even a soul most powerfully struggling for unity can never completely achieve it. But any work that I do with a united soul reacts upon my soul, acts in the direction of new and greater unification, leads me, though by all sorts of detours, to a *steadier* unity than was the preceding one. Thus man ultimately reaches a point where he can rely upon his soul, because its unity is now so great that it overcomes contradiction with effortless ease. Vigilance, of course, is necessary even then, but it is a relaxed vigilance.

On one of the days of the Hanukkah feast, Rabbi Nahum, the son of the rabbi of Rishyn,[1] entered the House of Study at a time when he was not expected, and found his disciples playing checkers, as was the custom on those days. When they saw the zaddik they were embarrassed and stopped playing. But he gave them a kindly nod and asked: 'Do you know the rules of the game of checkers?' And when they did not reply for shyness he himself gave the answer: 'I shall

[1] i.e., Ružyn (District of Kiev). Rabbi Israel of Rishyn was the founder of the famous 'Dynasty of Sadagora'.

tell you the rules of the game of checkers. The first is that one must not make two moves at once. The second is that one may only move forward and not backward. And the third is that when one has reached the last row, one may move wherever one likes.'

However, what is meant by unification of the soul would be thoroughly misunderstood if 'soul' were taken to mean anything but the whole man, body and spirit together. The soul is not really united, unless all bodily energies, all the limbs of the body, are united. The Baal-Shem interpreted the biblical passage 'Whatsoever thy hands find to do, do it with thy might' to the effect that the deeds one does should be done with every limb, i.e., even the whole of man's physical being should participate in it, no part of him should remain outside. A man who thus becomes a unit of body and spirit—he is the man whose work is all of a piece.

IV. BEGINNING WITH ONESELF

Once when Rabbi Yitzhak of Vorki was playing host to certain prominent men of Israel, they discussed the value to a household of an honest and efficient servant. They said that a good servant made for good management and cited Joseph at whose hands everything prospered. Rabbi Yitzhak objected. 'I once thought that too,' he said. 'But then my teacher showed me that everything depends on the master of the house. You see, in my youth my wife gave me a great deal of trouble, and though I myself put up with her as best I could, I was sorry for the servants. So I went to my teacher, Rabbi David of Lelov, and asked him whether I should oppose my wife. All he said was: "Why do you speak to me? Speak to yourself!" I thought over these words for quite a while before I understood them. But I did understand them when I recalled a certain saying of the Baal-Shem: "There is thought, speech and action. Thought corresponds to one's wife, speech to one's children, and action to one's servants. Whoever straightens himself out in regard to all three will find that everything prospers at his hands." Then I understood what my teacher had meant: everything depended on myself.'

This story touches upon one of the deepest and most difficult problems of our life: the true origin of conflict between man and man.

Manifestations of conflict are usually explained

either by the motives of which the quarrelling parties are conscious as the occasion of their quarrel, and by the objective situations and processes which underlie these motives and in which both parties are involved; or, proceeding analytically, we try to explore the unconscious complexes to which these motives relate like mere symptoms of an illness to the organic disturbances themselves. Hasidic teaching coincides with this conception in that it, too, derives the problematics of external from that of internal life. But it differs in two essential points, one fundamental and one practical, the latter of which is even more important than the former.

The fundamental difference is that hasidic teaching is not concerned with the exploration of particular psychical complications, but envisages man as a whole. This is, however, by no means a quantitative difference. For the hasidic conception springs from the realization that the isolation of elements and partial processes from the whole hinders the comprehension of the whole, and that real transformation, real restoration, at first of the single person and subsequently of the relationship between him and his fellow-men, can only be achieved by the comprehension of the whole as a whole. (Putting it paradoxically: the search for the centre of gravity shifts it and thereby frustrates the whole attempt at over-coming the problematics involved.) This is not to say that there is no need to consider all the phenomena of the soul; but no one of them should be made so much the centre of attention as if everything else could be derived from it; rather, they should all be made starting-points—not singly but in their vital connection.

The practical difference is that in Hasidism man is not treated as an object of examination but is called upon to 'straighten himself out'. At first, a man should himself realize that conflict-situations between himself and others are nothing but the effects of conflict-situations in his own soul; then he should try to overcome this inner conflict, so that afterwards he may go out to his fellow-men and enter into new, transformed relationships with them.

Man naturally tries to avoid this decisive reversal—extremely repugnant to him in his accustomed relationship to the world—by referring him who thus appeals to him, or his own soul, if it is his soul that makes the appeal, to the fact that every conflict involves two parties and that, if he is expected to turn his attention from the external to his own internal conflict, his opponent should be expected to do the same. But just this perspective, in which a man sees himself only as an individual contrasted with other individuals, and not as a genuine person, whose transformation helps towards the transformation of the world, contains the fundamental error which hasidic teaching denounces. The essential thing is to begin with oneself, and at this moment a man has nothing in the world to care about than this beginning. Any other attitude would distract him from what he is about to begin, weaken his initiative, and thus frustrate the entire bold undertaking.

Rabbi Bunam taught:

'Our sages say: "Seek peace in your own place."
You cannot find peace anywhere save in your own
self. In the psalm we read: "There is no peace in my
bones because of my sin." When a man has made
peace within himself, he will be able to make peace in
the whole world.'

However, the story from which I started does not
confine itself to pointing out the true origin of external
conflicts, i.e., the internal conflict, in a general way.
The quoted saying of the Baal-Shem states exactly in
what the decisive inner conflict consists. It is the conflict between three principles in man's being and life,
the principle of thought, the principle of speech, and
the principle of action. The origin of all conflict between me and my fellow-men is that I do not say
what I mean, and that I do not do what I say. For this
confuses and poisons, again and again and in increasing
measure, the situation between myself and the other
man, and I, in my internal disintegration, am no longer
able to master it but, contrary to all my illusions, have
become its slave. By our contradiction, our lie, we
foster conflict-situations and give them power over us
until they enslave us. From here, there is no way out
but by the crucial realization: Everything depends on
myself, and the crucial decision: I will straighten myself out.

But in order that a man may be capable of this great
feat, he must find his way from the casual, accessory
elements of his existence to his own self: he must find

his own self, not the trivial ego of the egotistic individual, but the deeper self of the person living in a relationship to the world. And that is also contrary to everything we are accustomed to.

I will close this chapter with an old jest as retold by a zaddik.

Rabbi Hanokh told this story:

There was once a man who was very stupid. When he got up in the morning it was so hard for him to find his clothes that at night he almost hesitated to go to bed for thinking of the trouble he would have on waking. One evening he finally made a great effort, took paper and pencil and as he undressed noted down exactly where he put everything he had on. The next morning, very well pleased with himself, he took the slip of paper in his hand and read: 'cap'—there it was, he set it on his head; 'pants'—there they lay, he got into them; and so it went until he was fully dressed. 'That's all very well, but now where am I myself?' he asked in great consternation. 'Where in the world am I?' He looked and looked, but it was a vain search; he could not find himself. 'And that is how it is with us,' said the rabbi.

V. NOT TO BE PREOCCUPIED
WITH ONESELF

Rabbi Hayyim of Zans[1] had married his son to the daughter of Rabbi Eliezer. The day after the wedding he visited the father of the bride and said: 'Now that we are related I feel close to you and can tell you what is eating at my heart. Look! My hair and beard have grown white, and I have not yet atoned!'

'O my friend,' replied Rabbi Eliezer, 'you are thinking only of yourself. How about forgetting yourself and thinking of the world?'

What is said here, seems to contradict everything I have hitherto reported of the teachings of Hasidism. We have heard that everyone should search his own heart, choose his particular way, bring about the unity of his being, begin with himself; and now we are told that man should forget himself. But if we examine this injunction more closely, we find that it is not only consistent with the others, but fits into the whole as a necessary link, as a necessary stage, in its particular place. One need only ask one question: 'What for?' What am I to choose my particular way for? What am I to unify my being for? The reply is: Not for my own sake. This is why the previous injunction was: to *begin* with oneself. To begin with oneself, but not to end with oneself; to start from oneself, but not to aim

_____
[1] i.e., Nowy Sacz in Western Galicia.

31

at oneself; to comprehend oneself, but not to be pre-
occupied with oneself.

We see a zaddik, a wise, pious, kindly man, reproach himself in his old age for not yet having performed the true turning. The reply given him is
apparently prompted by the opinion that he greatly
overrates his sins and greatly underrates the penance he
has already done. But what Rabbi Eliezer says, goes
beyond this. He says, in quite a general sense: 'Do not
keep worrying about what you have done wrong, but
apply the soul power you are now wasting on self-
reproach, to such active relationship to the world as
you are destined for. You should not be occupied with
yourself but with the world.'

First of all, we should properly understand what is
said here about turning. It is known that turning
stands in the centre of the Jewish conception of the
way of man. Turning is capable of renewing a man
from within and changing his position in God's world,
so that he who turns is seen standing above the perfect
zaddik, who does not know the abyss of sin. But turning means here something much greater than repen-
tance and acts of penance; it means that by a reversal
of his whole being, a man who had been lost in the
maze of selfishness, where he had always set himself
as his goal, finds a way to God, that is, a way to the
fulfilment of the particular task for which he, this
particular man, has been destined by God. Re-
pentance can only be an incentive to such active
reversal; he who goes on fretting himself with re-

pentance, he who tortures himself with the idea that his acts of penance are not sufficient, witholds his best energies from the work of reversal. In a sermon on the Day of Atonement, the Rabbi of Ger warned against self-torture:

'He who has done ill and talks about it and thinks about it all the time does not cast the base thing he did out of his thoughts, and whatever one thinks, therein one is, one's soul is wholly and utterly in what one thinks, and so he dwells in baseness. He will certainly not be able to turn, for his spirit will grow coarse and his heart stubborn, and in addition to this he may be overcome by gloom. What would you? Rake the muck this way, rake the muck that way—it will always be muck. Have I sinned, or have I not sinned—what does Heaven get out of it? In the time I am brooding over it I could be stringing pearls for the delight of Heaven. That is why it is written: "Depart from evil and do good"—turn wholly away from evil, do not dwell upon it, and do good. You have done wrong? Then counteract it by doing right.'

But the significance of our story goes beyond this. He who tortures himself incessantly with the idea that he has not yet sufficiently atoned, is essentially concerned with the salvation of his soul, with his personal fate in eternity. By rejecting this aim, Hasidism merely draws a conclusion from the teachings of Judaism generally. One of the main points in which Christianity differs from Judaism is that it makes each man's salvation his highest aim. Judaism regards each man's soul as a serving member of God's Creation which, by man's work, is to become the Kingdom of God; thus no soul has its object in itself, in its own salvation. True, each is to know itself, purify itself, perfect itself, but not for its own sake—neither for the sake of its temporal happiness nor for that of its eternal bliss—but for the sake of the work which it is destined to perform upon the world.

The pursuit of one's own salvation is here regarded merely as the sublimest form of self-intending. Self-intending is what Hasidism rejects most emphatically, and quite especially in the case of the man who has found and developed his own self. Rabbi Bunam said: It is written: 'Now Korah took'. What did he take? He wanted to take himself—therefore, nothing he did could be of any worth. This is why Bunam contrasted the eternal Korah with the eternal Moses, the 'humble' man, whose doings are not aimed at himself. Rabbi Bunam taught: 'In every generation the soul of Moses and the soul of Korah return. But if once, in days to come, the soul of Korah is willing to subject itself to the soul of Moses, Korah will be redeemed.'

Rabbi Bunam thus sees, as it were, the history of mankind on its road to redemption as a process involving two kinds of men, the proud who, if sometimes in the sublimest form, think of themselves, and the humble, who in all matters think of the world. Only when pride subjects itself to humility can it be redeemed; and only when it is redeemed, can the world be redeemed.

After Rabbi Bunam's death, one of his disciples—the aforementioned Rabbi of Ger, from whose sermon on the Day of Atonement I quoted a few sentences—remarked: 'Rabbi Bunam had the keys to all the firmaments. And why not? A man who does not think of himself is given all the keys.'

The greatest of Rabbi Bunam's disciples, a truly tragic figure among the zaddikim, Rabbi Mendel of Kotzk, once said to his congregation: 'What, after all, do I demand of you? Only three things: not to look furtively outside yourselves, not to look furtively into others, and not to aim at yourselves.' That is to say: firstly, everyone should preserve and hallow his own soul in its own particularity and in its own place, and not envy the particularity and place of others; secondly, everyone should respect the secret in the soul of his fellow-man, and not, with brazen curiosity, intrude upon it and take advantage of it; and thirdly, everyone, in his relationship to the world, should be careful not to set himself as his aim.

VI. HERE WHERE ONE STANDS

Rabbi Bunam used to tell young men who came to him for the first time the story of Rabbi Eizik, son of Rabbi Yekel of Cracow. After many years of great poverty which had never shaken his faith in God, he dreamed someone bade him look for a treasure in Prague, under the bridge which leads to the king's palace. When the dream recurred a third time, Rabbi Eizik prepared for the journey and set out for Prague. But the bridge was guarded day and night and he did not dare to start digging. Nevertheless he went to the bridge every morning and kept walking around it until evening. Finally the captain of the guards, who had been watching him, asked in a kindly way whether he was looking for something or waiting for somebody. Rabbi Eizik told him of the dream which had brought him here from a faraway country. The captain laughed: 'And so to please the dream, you poor fellow wore out your shoes to come here! As for having faith in dreams, if I had had it, I should have had to get going when a dream once told me to go to Cracow and dig for treasure under the stove in the room of a Jew—Eizik, son of Yekel, that was the name! Eizik, son of Yekel! I can just imagine what it would be like, how I should have to try every house over there, where one half of the Jews are named Eizik and the other Yekel!' And he laughed again. Rabbi Eizik bowed, travelled home, dug up the treasure from under the stove, and built the House of

Prayer which is called 'Reb Eizik Reb Yekel's Shul'.

'Take this story to heart,' Rabbi Bunam used to add, 'and make what it says your own: There is something you cannot find anywhere in the world, not even at the zaddik's, and there is, nevertheless, a place where you can find it.'

This, too, is a very old story, known from several popular literatures, but thoroughly reshaped by Hasidism. It has not merely—in a superficial sense—been transplanted into the Jewish sphere, it has been recast by the hasidic melody in which it has been told; but even this is not decisive: the decisive change is that it has become, so to speak, transparent, and that a hasidic truth is shining through its words. It has not had a 'moral' appended to it, but the sage who retold it had at last discovered its true meaning and made it apparent.

There is something that can only be found in one place. It is a great treasure, which may be called the fulfilment of existence. The place where this treasure can be found is the place on which one stands.

Most of us achieve only at rare moments a clear realization of the fact that they have never tasted the fulfilment of existence, that their life does not participate in true, fulfilled existence, that, as it were, it passes true existence by. We nevertheless feel the deficiency at every moment, and in some measure strive to find —somewhere—what we are seeking. Somewhere, in some province of the world or of the mind, except where we stand, where we have been set—but it is

37

there and nowhere else that the treasure can be found. The environment which I feel to be the natural one, the situation which has been assigned to me as my fate, the things that happen to me day after day, the things that claim me day after day—these contain my essential task and such fulfilment of existence as is open to me. It is said of a certain Talmudic master that the paths of heaven were as bright to him as the streets of his native town. Hasidism inverts the order: It is a greater thing if the streets of a man's native town are as bright to him as the paths of heaven. For it is here, where we stand, that we should try to make shine the light of the hidden divine life.

If we had power over the ends of the earth, it would not give us that fulfilment of existence which a quiet devoted relationship to nearby life can give us. If we knew the secrets of the upper worlds, they would not allow us so much actual participation in true existence as we can achieve by performing, with holy intent, a task belonging to our daily duties. Our treasure is hidden beneath the hearth of our own home.

The Baal-Shem teaches that no encounter with a being or a thing in the course of our life lacks a hidden significance. The people we live with or meet with, the animals that help us with our farmwork, the soil we till, the materials we shape, the tools we use, they all contain a mysterious spiritual substance which depends on us for helping it towards its pure form, its perfection. If we neglect this spiritual substance sent across our path, if we think only in terms of momentary purposes, without developing a genuine relationship to the beings and things in whose life we ought to take part, as they in ours, then we shall ourselves be debarred from true, fulfilled existence. It is my conviction that this doctrine is essentially true. The highest culture of the soul remains basically arid and barren unless, day by day, waters of life pour forth into the soul from those little encounters to which we give their due; the most formidable power is intrinsically powerlessness unless it maintains a secret covenant with these contacts, both humble and helpful, with strange, and yet near, being.

Some religions do not regard our sojourn on earth as true life. They either teach that everything appearing to us here is mere appearance, behind which we should penetrate, or that it is only a forecourt of the true world, a forecourt which we should cross without paying much attention to it. Judaism, on the contrary, teaches that what a man does now and here with holy intent is no less important, no less true—being a terrestrial indeed, but none the less factual, link with divine being—than the life in the world to come. This doctrine has found its fullest expression in Hasidism.

Rabbi Hanokh said: 'The other nations too believe that there are two worlds. They too say: "In the other world." The difference is this: They think that the two are separate and severed, but Israel professes that the two worlds are essentially one and shall in fact become one.'

In their true essence, the two worlds are one. They

only have, as it were, moved apart. But they shall again become one, as they are in their true essence. Man was created for the purpose of unifying the two worlds. He contributes towards this unity by holy living, in relationship to the world in which he has been set, at the place on which he stands.

Once they told Rabbi Pinhas of the great misery among the needy. He listened, sunk in grief. Then he raised his head. 'Let us draw God into the world,' he cried, 'and all need will be quenched.'

But is this possible, to draw God into the world? Is this not an arrogant, presumptious idea? How dare the lowly worm touch upon a matter which depends entirely on God's grace: how much of Himself He will vouchsafe to His creation?

Here again, Jewish doctrine is opposed to that of other religions, and again it is in Hasidism that it has found its fullest expression. God's grace consists precisely in this, that he wants to let himself be won by man, that he places himself, so to speak, into man's hands. God wants to come to his world, but he wants to come to it through man. This is the mystery of our existence, the superhuman chance of mankind.

'Where is the dwelling of God?'

This is the question with which the Rabbi of Kotzk surprised a number of learned men who happened to be visiting him.

They laughed at him: 'What a thing to ask! Is not the whole world full of his glory?'

Then he answered his own question:

'God dwells wherever man lets him in.'

This is the ultimate purpose: to let God in. But we can let him in only where we really stand, where we live, where we live a true life. If we maintain holy intercourse with the little world entrusted to us, if we help the holy spiritual substance to accomplish itself in that section of Creation in which we are living, then we are establishing, in this our place, a dwelling for the Divine Presence.